TRAIN WRECK 2016
© 2016 by Paul Covell

Table of Contents

Foreword

He is brash. He is bold. He is in love with himself. He is a New Yorker. However, will the Donald sell in the South, or even in New York City? Is Donald Trump the end for the Republican Party? What if Trump does not want to be president? Does that explain his baffling rants against minorities? How many of us thought that Trump did not understand the effect of his statements at the start of the 2016 Primary Campaign? The truth is that he knew exactly what he was doing.

Trump ran an unscripted, one man, reality show that appealed to the base instincts of the Tea Party rebels in the Republican Party. Trump's message is neither nuanced nor restrained. It is balls-out testosterone, garnished with prejudice, racism, xenophobia, and jingoism. Trump in 2016 is a reprise of George Wallace in 1968. The difference is that Wallace was genuine, and more honest about his flawed vision for America.

In his 1963 Inaugural Speech as Governor Elect of Alabama, Wallace bared his soul. *"In the name of the greatest people that have ever trod this earth, I draw the line in the dust and toss the gauntlet before the feet of tyranny, and I say segregation now, segregation tomorrow, segregation forever."*

Wallace led the American Independent (*"America First"*) Party, and appealed to the same malcontents that Trump courts in 2016. There was no real debate in the 2016 GOP Primary. Trump dispatched his foils with one-liners. Jeb Bush, the darling of the conservative establishment, fell to the epithet of *"Low Energy"*—a not so thinly veiled hint that, by contrast, the Donald sported *"Huevos Mas Grandes"*. Trump dismissed Marco Rubio, another establishment darling, as "Little Marco", suggesting *"Huevos Juveniles"*.

Democrats fared no better. Rodham-Clinton suffered the sobriquet *"Crooked Hillary"*. In a move that would alienate all of our tribal instincts and national sense of decency, Trumped dubbed Elizabeth Warren *"Pocahontas"*. Hillary branded Trump as *"Dangerously Incoherent"*. The difference between the racism of Wallace and Trump is that the Donald equivocates to mask his virulence. Wallace never faked political correctness. Ironically, Trump feigns political incorrectness.

How did Republican Leadership receive Trump's conduct? It was almost as if a parent or guardian had to apologize for a rambunctious toddler flailing about in a China Shop. The China Shop of course is the Republican Party, but threatens to be the Nation. One could almost hear House Speaker Ryan and Senate Majority Leader

McConnell promising, *"He'll get better in a few months"*. *"He'll grow out of it."* Finally, McConnell had to say, *"I am not commenting on the presidential candidates today."*

Advice from Paul Ryan and Ted Cruz to Convention Delegates, *"Vote your conscience."* The list of those boycotting the 2016 GOP Cleveland Convention is impressive. Papa Bush, George W. Bush, Jeb Bush, Mitt Romney, John McCain, and John Kasich as Ohio host Governor. Speaker Ryan had to attend as Convention Chair. Ryan offered to step aside, if Trump wanted to stage-manage the Convention with his own Chair.

Trump's so-called pivot to General Election Campaign mode seemed more of a divot. After repeatedly bashing District Court Judge Gonzalo Curiel for not dismissing a Class Action Lawsuit against Trump University, Trump declared that it was important to protect the judiciary [from an overbearing Executive Branch]. Trump's attack against the judge was an example of linear logic premised on a non-sequitur.

Trump railed against Mexico in his primary rants. *"Not sending us the best"*. Sending us *"rapists"*. Trump's solution to the lawsuit. *"Build a Wall"*. Ergo, the judge is prejudiced. To hold the attention of wavering supporters, Trump incanted his mantra and major premise of dysfunctional logic. *"I'm building a wall."* *"I'm building a wall."* Ergo, anyone with Mexican heritage could not fairly rule on a lawsuit against Trump University. QED. Trump's tortured logic allows him to insult every group, and then claim that a member of the aggrieved group cannot fairly evaluate Trump's shenanigans.

Mitch McConnell told us all we need to know about Trump. *"He needs someone highly experienced and very knowledgeable [for Vice President] because it's pretty obvious he doesn't know a lot about the issues."* That, however, does not mean that Trump does not strategize. Trump's attack on Judge Curiel has been a long time in the making. Trump's foray against Mexico was a predicate for the attack on the judge, who would not dismiss the lawsuit against Trump University. After all, Trump is *"building a wall"*.

In Trump logic, it is reasonable to conclude that the judge is a Trump-hater because the judge's parents came from Mexico. Some condemn Trump because the attack on the judiciary has no obvious connection to the issues of the campaign. If the candidate actively participated in defrauding the vulnerable and the gullible, however, why would that not be relevant to the measure of the man who would be president? Trump's elaborate attack on the judge highlights Trump's realization that the lawsuit against Trump University may have serious consequences for the man and the candidate.

The Trump saga of 2016 underscores the imploding nature of today's Republican Party. The idealism of the 1850s is long gone. President Lyndon Johnson presciently remarked that his support of the *Voting Rights Act of 1965* would lose the South for the Democratic Party. From 1868 to 1948, the South voted solidly with the Democrats. Strom Thurmond (D-SC) led a Dixiecrat revolt and walkout from the 1948 Democratic Convention in a festering protest over adoption of civil rights planks in the Party Platform.

What started as a protest by white delegates in 1948 became a stampede of white voters after 1965. Democrats who could not accept Civil Rights joined the Republican Party in droves. States' Rights was the jingle. Do States and erstwhile, majority, white voters really have the right to discriminate against minority voters in derogation of the Fourteenth Amendment?

Trump is the flawed leader of a flawed Party that has no heart or soul. GOP Leaders evaluate Donald Trump in 2016 mainly on his ability to affect down-ballot races. Speaker Ryan does not want to lose his comfortable GOP majority in the House. Mitch McConnell fears losing majority control in the Senate. Control of Government, Power, and Money motivate the political parties.

It is as though Tammany Hall runs our national government for the patronage. There will be many twists and turns in the 2016 race. Trump's divot may become a true pivot. In the general election, Trump may run away from the bigot he was in the primary. Trump will use the Teleprompter to deliver scripted speeches devoid of attacks on women, minorities, Moslems, and judges. Tea Partiers and rednecks will be bored. Ryan and McConnell will be delighted. It is the beginning of the end for the GOP.

Joe Scarborough (*"Morning Joe"*) repeatedly warned Republicans in June 2016 of the gathering crisis that Trump presents to the GOP as a viable political party. House Speaker Ryan (R-WI) and Senate Majority Leader McConnell (R-KY) seem paralyzed by the grass roots support that Trump won in the GOP Primaries.

By not vigorously condemning Trump's bigotry and racism during the Primary, Ryan and McConnell have made it more difficult to take corrective action during the General Election Campaign. By allowing Trump to represent the GOP in the General Election, Ryan and McConnell are risking a national cataclysm, or at least a Party debacle.

What if Trump is able to muster a majority of electoral votes in a four-way race (R, D, L, and G)? If a fractured election result (where Libertarians' percentage of votes is in double digits) throws the decision to the House of Representatives, Trump could emerge as Commander-in-Chief in what surely will develop into a Greek Tragedy.

Amazingly, the method of weighting Electoral College Votes may result in a Trump victory. The candidate does not need to win fifty states, only 270 Electoral Votes. Eleven largest states can carry the election. California, New York, and Illinois may be out of reach to Republicans as heavily Blue states in 2016.

Trump will concentrate instead on Florida, North Carolina, Pennsylvania, Michigan, Ohio, and Indiana. Trump can rely on Red States of Alaska, Alabama, Arkansas, Arizona, Georgia, Kentucky Louisiana, Mississippi, Montana, South Carolina, Tennessee, Texas, and West Virginia. The battle will rage in the swing states of Florida, Virginia, North Carolina, Colorado, New Mexico, Nevada, and New Hampshire.

Trump's message, which worked for angry GOP Primary voters, nonetheless may appeal to General Election voters on Four Decisive Emotional Themes: (1) Americans' Loss of Jobs and Manufacturing capability, (2). Immigration of Insufficiently Vetted and Possibly Dangerous Persons, (3) National Defense and Security, and (4) Hillary's emails and Bill's pay to play charity. The 2016 Election will not turn on cerebral issues.

If it did, Hillary Clinton, aided by Barack Obama, would prevail. The 2016 election will turn on emotional, gut issues. People will vote their instincts. The White Majority is losing its grip on the helm as demographics marches inexorably towards a rainbow electorate. The Middle Class is dying as wealth exports to low-cost manufacturing centers in Asia. America's vaunted military establishment stagnates in Afghanistan and Iraq. The entire world worries about the chaos in Syria and the flood of refugees to Jordan, Turkey, and Europe.

If the Clinton's do not sever all ties with the Clinton Global Initiative, the Presidency of Hillary Clinton will suffer more investigations than that of William Jefferson Clinton.

Chapter 1.
GOP Abandons High Ideals

There was a spirit of fairness and equality trying to break out of the institutional oppression in the United States in the 1850's, when the enterprising Lehman Brothers established themselves as up and coming cotton brokers in Montgomery, Alabama. Lehman Brothers immigrated to America from Germany, and thought their business here could grow and prosper indefinitely along with the development of their young adopted homeland.

Lehman Brothers became a symbol of the immigrant success story that could never fail so long as the immigrant persevered and the Nation succeeded. America's original sin of slavery festered under the protection of the Constitution of the land of the brave and the home of the free.

Our Founders knew there was an existential problem with slavery even before the birth of the Nation. They feared the cure might be worse than the disease. If Connecticut, Massachusetts, New York, and Pennsylvania insisted on abolishing slavery, would Virginia, Maryland, Georgia, and the Carolinas refuse to join the proposed Union?

Slavery became a way of life and death in the young Nation. So important to its exploiters and sponsors, the issue of slavery raged around the vital question of admission of new states to the Union. The House of Representatives reflected the relative state population of eligible voters: i. e., white, male, property owners. Southern House Members started to lag behind their northern counterparts in relative numbers, as the population of northern states grew faster. Slaves counted as three fifths of a free man for allotting seats in the House. Const., Art. 1, § 2, ¶ 3.

Every new state sent two new members to the Senate, which became the focus and locus of the battle for state sovereignty, and for the knockdown, drag out battle over slavery. If Free States joined the Union, without admission of paired Slave States, the House and the Senate soon would vote slavery down as an archaic, evil institution.

House Speaker Henry Clay (D-KY) insisted to northerners that slavery must preserve an equal voice in the Senate, if business were to go forward in regular order. In 1820, the *Missouri Compromise* provided for Maine to join the Union as a Free State, with Missouri admitted as a Slave State. Future extension of slavery was limited to the latitude of the southern border of Missouri.

The *Kansas-Nebraska Act* (1854) shredded the *Great Compromise*. (Kansas admitted as a Slave State). The gathering discord over the spread of slavery led to the formation of the Republican Party, and paved the way for the Civil War. Abolitionists could not abide with the perpetuation of slavery. Horace Greeley founded and edited the New York Tribune.

Greeley and others provided the spark that led to the formation in 1854 of the Republican Party, which advocated principles of free labor (as opposed to slave labor) and free land (as opposed to slave estates).

Republicans championed small businesses, small farms, labor, and the end to slavery.

The Tribune proclaimed the virtues of the Republican Party. In 1856, John Frémont led the Party under the banner: *Free soil, Free men, Frémont.* James Buchanan (D-PA) prevailed. Abraham Lincoln led the nascent party to victory in 1860 with a meager plurality of 39.8 percent of the popular vote, diluted by the presence on the ballot of two Democratic Tickets (southern and northern) and the Constitutional Party.

Lincoln handily won the Electoral College with 180 out of 303. Only John Quincy Adams (selected by the House) won with fewer popular votes in 1824, with 30.9% to Andrew Jackson's 41.4%. Jackson won many more electoral votes than did Adams, but lacked a majority. Henry Clay and William Crawford siphoned off additional popular votes in 1824.

In the beginning, Republicans had a heart and a soul. Democrats in the South embraced slavery. A divided Nation elected Abraham Lincoln President in November 1860. Before Lincoln took the oath of office (never mind take any action adverse to the South, or propose to abolish or burden slavery), South Carolina seceded from the Union on December 20, 1860.

The rest of the South soon followed. Buchanan would remain President until March 1861. Buchanan considered secession illegal, but took no action against the eleven states that seceded. Lincoln had to be careful that the train carrying him to Washington, D C, for inauguration did not pass through rebel territory. When Maryland toyed with the idea of secession, Lincoln had to take decisive action to prevent the capital from isolation in hostile territory. The State of Maryland and the City of Baltimore chafed at the idea of northern troops marching through Baltimore to defend Washington.

The privilege of the writ of habeas corpus shall not be suspended, unless when in cases of Rebellion or invasion the public safety may require it. U.S. Constitution, Article I, § 9.

The Nation's Founders instinctively understood the need for the Executive to put down a rebellion summarily, and without legal niceties. U.S. Supreme Court Chief Justice Roger B. Taney wanted to make legal process mandatory even during a rebellion. Taney was a Democrat and a native of Maryland, who opposed Lincoln's policies. The Governor of Maryland ordered destruction of the rail bridges and telegraph lines linking Baltimore with the north, thinking that blocking the passage of federal troops would pacify the mob of insurrectionists in Baltimore.

This followed the murder of several members of the Massachusetts Sixth Regiment marching through Baltimore. Lincoln imposed martial law on Maryland, and ordered the military to suspend the writ of habeas corpus as may be necessary. The Army arrested John Merryman for destroying the bridges and cutting lines pursuant to the Governor's order. The U.S. District Court in Baltimore issued a writ of habeas corpus. The Army balked. Chief Justice Taney, sitting as a Circuit Appellate Judge, upheld the writ. *Ex parte Merryman.*

Lincoln ordered the Army to ignore Taney's order to produce Merryman in Court. Since Taney issued the order as a Circuit Judge, the President technically was not at odds with the Supreme Court. The Army restored the bridges and telegraph lines connecting Baltimore with the North. Lincoln acted logically in face of imminent threat. The South intended to occupy the capital.

If the Nation were to survive, troops from the North must transit through Baltimore to relieve the capital. Lincoln reasoned that he had the power and duty to suspend the Constitution in war- torn sectors, where civil government was not operational or was dysfunctional because of mob influence. Congress authorized *Suspension of Habeas Corpus* in 1863. The power of the President to order the military to try civilians for interfering with the war effort was defined in *Ex parte Milligan* (1866) 71 U.S. 22. Civilians have the right to trial in civil courts, where civil government is operational.

John Wilkes Booth, a native of Maryland, shot Lincoln at Ford's Theater, Washington, April 14, 1865. Booth vehemently opposed abolition of slavery. Republicans in Congress and in State Legislatures brought freedom and citizenship to the oppressed through adoption of the 13th, 14th, and 15th Amendments to the Constitution. Everyone born within its borders and subject to its laws was at birth a citizen of the United States and the State where they reside. The Civil Rights Laws enacted in the 1870s, now classified under 42 USC §§ 1981-1985.

There was a genuine burst of freedom and equality for all during the ten years following the end of the Civil War. Blacks won seats in Congress. In 1876, the Republicans abandoned the struggle. Rutherford B. Hayes (R-OH) and Samuel Tilden (D-NY) tied in the closest election in American History.

Both political parties desperately searched for the last electoral vote to break the tie of 184 or 185. Tilden won 50.92% of the popular vote. Twenty electoral votes in four states were under legal challenge. Recently admitted Colorado was unable or unwilling to hold a statewide election, so the legislature cast the state's votes for Hayes.

Commissions debated on how to allocate the vote. Republicans threatened to resume reconstruction and deploy federal troops in some Southern States.

The Nation was on the verge of another Civil War. Hayes and Tilden made a cynical pact with the devil in 1877. Tilden agreed to recognize Hayes as President, and withdraw all electoral vote challenges. Hayes agreed to allow the Democrats to have free reign in the South. The Republican Party sold its soul for a bowl of porridge. Blacks would have to wait a while for equality.

Jim Crow ruled the South from 1878 to 1968. The post-Civil War Amendments to the Constitution withered on the vine. The federal government ignored 42 USC §§ 1981-1985 for more than seventy years. No more blacks elected to Congress from the South until after the *Voting Rights Act of 1965*. Segregation was enforced. Real property deeds were open to bans on selling to blacks until outlawed in 1948 by *Shelley v. Kraemer*, (334 U.S. 1).

The South voted solidly for Democrats until 1948, when Strom Thurmond bolted the Democratic Convention to protest adoption of civil rights planks. *Plessy v. Ferguson*, 173 U.S. 537, upheld segregation in 1896. (*"We consider the underlying fallacy of the plaintiff's argument to consist of the assumption that the enforced separation of the two races stamps the colored race with a badge of inferiority."*) p. 551.

Brown v. Board of Education of Topeka, Kansas, (1954) 447 U.S. 483, held unanimously that separate is inherently unequal. The South answered by sponsoring Private Schools. After the *Voting Rights Act of 1965*, Southern Democrats fled to the open arms of the Republican Party. No worries. Donald J. Trump promises to create jobs for African Americans and all Americans.

Chapter 2.
Trump Promised Never to Lie to You

At a rally in Charlotte, NC, on August 18, 2016, Trump promised never to lie to you. That, of course, was a bold-faced lie. Trump's entire campaign, and the preparation for it, is one colossal lie. Remember Trump in 2011, as Birther-in-Chief, telling the American People that President Obama was not born in the U.S. Trump lied when he claimed he sent investigators to Hawaii to gather evidence that President Obama's birth certificate was phony.

When someone feels it is necessary to promise never to lie, that is a proof that they lie whenever it suits them. Trump brags about not being a politician. Trump, however, lies more than any politician in U.S. history. Trump's entire life is one continuous lie. He took the marital forever pledge three times. He obsesses over Americans loss of jobs, but he makes all of Trump products for sale in the U.S. in China, Europe, and anywhere but the U.S.

On August 17, 2016, he suddenly became an advocate for the African American community. The location was West Bend, Wisconsin. The audience reflected the racial composition of West Bend at 99% white. Forty miles away, the African American community in Milwaukee is suffering unrest and alienation, but the Donald did not want to go there. It is a travesty that Trump is on the ballot as a Republican. He is not a conservative. However, that does not make him a progressive.

Trump stands on the far edge of the GOP, out in the mist and darkness, where Neo-Nazis furtively pass by Birthers, White Supremacists, Nationalists, Wall Builders, Anti-Semites, Misogynists, Know-Nothings, Know-It-Alls, and Fanatics who are convinced that civilization has no effect on Climate Change.

Trump's inner compass is oriented toward conspiracy theories and threats to the homeland by immigrants and minorities. Trump believes in Breitbart News. That may explain why Trump brought in Breitbart's Chairman, Stephen Bannon, as CEO of the Trump Campaign on 8/16/16. Bannon has no experience in managing a campaign. There is only one qualification needed. Bannon must let Trump be Trump. Expect more lies. At the same time that Trump promised not to lie, he said he regretted some of the things he said in the past, without describing the offensive speech or the persons insulted. This is sort of a blank regret, where the individual offended can write in their name and the date of the insult.

John McCain could consider that Trump regrets rejecting McCain's Military Service because the North Vietnamese captured McCain. Meghan Kelly could consider that Trump regrets dissing her because she is a woman. Khisr Khan could consider that Trump regrets trying to humiliate a Gold Star Family. Pat Smith, mother of Sean Smith, could consider that Trump regrets exploiting her at the GOP Convention to blame Hillary for the Benghazi attack.

By the way, Richard J. Cross III, the person who prepared Pat Smith's speech, announced that he cannot vote for Trump. *"But the only prospect more terrifying than voting for Hillary Clinton is not voting for her."* Baltimore Sun 8/17/16. Paul Ryan could consider that Trump's initial refusal to endorse Ryan in the Wisconsin Primary was merely the result of bad vibes on Breitbart News.

African Americans could consider that Trump regrets pretending to advocate their cause. All Americans could consider that Trump regrets promising never to lie to them. Kelly Ayotte (R-NH), Ron Johnson (R-WI), and Pat Toomey (R-PA), could consider that Trump regrets putting their Senate Seats at risk. Melania Trump could consider that the Donald regrets allowing passages from a Michelle Obama speech to creep into Melania's GOP Convention Speech.

Hillary Clinton could consider that Trump regrets name-calling. Judge Curiel could consider that Trump regrets accusing the Judge of bias in not dismissing the lawsuit against Trump University, because of the Judge's Mexican heritage and Trump's plan to build a wall.

Chapter 3.
Captain Midnight Decoder Ring

Metropolitan Washington Old Time Radio Club (mwotrc.com) and Steven A. Kallis, Jr, offer that there were no decoder rings in old time radio, only decoder membership cards, first introduced in *Little Orphan Annie* in 1934, followed by Annie Decoder *Pins* in 1935. Decoder *Rings* came much later, after the term mysteriously came into use apparently before the ring thing came to market.

At all events, Rachel Maddow deserves humanitarian recognition greater than that given to Napoleon's Captain Bouchard, who in 1799, in the Nile Delta, discovered the *Rosetta Stone*, the key to deciphering Egyptian Hieroglyphs. On August 17, 2016, Rachel announced *the key to unveiling what makes Donald Trump tick.* What are his guiding lights? What does he really think? What is the source of his outlandish ideas? We cannot explain him in terms of conventional conservative principles.

We cannot use the template of William F. Buckley, Jr., to measure the Donald. Trump seems to be on the edge of the Republican Party, where the Conspiracy Kooks gather with the White Supremacists, Nationalists, neo-Nazis, anti-Semites, and, frankly, oddballs. We suspect that the Donald does some of his best work at midnight, surfing the internet for guidance, and then sending out zingers in tweets. Where does he get most of his tortured logic? Who is Trump's guru?

What possessed Trump to dismiss John McCain as a War Hero, because the North Vietnamese captured him? Why is Donald so prone to attack Republicans? One website broadcasts all of the strange views embraced by Trump. *Breitbart News* does not like John McCain. *Breitbart News* attacks Republicans as equal opportunity targets. Stephen Bannon is co-founder and Executive Chair of *Breitbart News*. On August 16, 2016, Trump reshuffled his campaign staff. He brought in Bannon from *Breitbart News*, presumably to let Donald be Donald. Trump was not happy with Paul Manafort's attempt to make Trump into a conventional politician.

Since Trump absorbs most of his radical ideas from *Breitbart News*, the *Drudge Report*, and Alex Jones' *Info Wars.com*, it does not take a genius to conclude that the Trump Campaign will play the Conspiracy Card to spice up a flagging campaign. He also brought in Kellyanne Conway to ride the hustings with the candidate, to woo women voters, and to explain the decline in poll numbers day by day.

Why Trump Can Never Be President

Trump started the campaign on a low level, and lost the majority of American Voters. When a candidate stoops to using epithets and insults, he cannot recover lost dignity. When Trump tries to tag the former Secretary of State with *'Crooked Hillary'*, he aims to detract from his opponent.

Lowbrow campaigning, however, detracts from the detractor. Imagine the shock in 1952 if Adlai Stevenson were to try to misbrand Dwight Eisenhower as *"Dopey Ike"*. There would have been a firestorm of protest.

There is a level, below which candidates cannot stoop. Even the surrogates cannot go to the gutter without besmirching their own candidate. There comes a time when the electorate stops believing anything said by the advocate of the tactics of the lowest common denominator. When Trump says, *'Believe me'*, no one does. That train has left the station [through the front wall with Trump at the throttle].

Amazingly, the Clintons present a barrage-balloon-size target for conspiracy theories. The U.S. State Department obviously has global reach. The Clinton Global Initiative (CGI) is a worldwide Foundation. Hillary Clinton was Secretary of State from 2009 to 2013. During Hillary's tenure at State, CGI took in hundreds of millions of dollars. Some of the contributors to CGI were looking for a favor from State. There is information that could fill many books in describing the Clintons' potential conflicts of interest. Peter Schweizer authored *Clinton Cash*, Harper Collins 2015, paperback 2016.

Schweizer is a contributor to breitbart.com. Trump hired Breitbart News Executive Chair Stephen Bannon. Conspiracy theories and pay for play allegations will explode from the Trump Campaign equal to the cannonade in Tchaikovsky's 1812 Overture. The Clintons must sever their ties with their charity, now known as *Clinton, Inc.*

The effort to bombard Hillary with *Clinton Cash*, however, will implode and crater upon the purveyors of tales from the dark side. There will be a factual basis for some of the allegations of pay to play. Showing actual quid pro quo will be difficult, if not impossible. The entire smear campaign will be for naught because a majority of the electorate no longer believes Donald Trump. Steve Bannon was instrumental in rallying the forces that drove Speaker John Boehner from office.

Bannon attacks Paul Ryan and Mitch McConnell with equal glee. *Blumberg News* casts Bannon as, *"This Man Is the Most Dangerous Political Operative in America"*. With this setup, it would seem that Clinton should lose. The electorate, however, has already decided that Trump is dangerous. Hiring Bannon, the most dangerous political operative, to spin conspiracy theories, does not make Trump appear any less dangerous.

Ironically, Trump would have put up a challenging campaign if had had listened to advocates like Rush Limbaugh, who are only slightly nuts. By going all in with Breitbart.com, Trump has left the majority shaking their heads in disbelief. It does not matter if Stephen Bannon spreads plausible conspiracy theories about the Clintons. Credibility is the issue.

Trump presented himself as pure Trump during the GOP 2016 primaries. The media gave Trump a million dollars of free press time. His primary opponents ran out of cash, and dropped out of the race. Name-calling, however, will not inspire the General Electorate.

Trump as pure Trump will not fly in the General. Stephen Bannon and Breitbart News can spin all the Clinton Cash, conspiracies theories they want, it will not help. A majority of the electorate has concluded that the Donald is not fit to be Commander-In-Chief. A campaign based mainly on the opponent's negatives ultimately will implode.

The GOP in general is leaving the American People far behind in the Right Wing crusade to bring down Hillary Clinton. House Republicans figuratively were foaming at the prospect of the FBI recommending an indictment against Hillary for alleged mishandling of classified State Department information on her home email server. FBI Director James Comey announced that no reasonable prosecutor would prosecute her, despite Rudy Giuliani's hysterical rant to the contrary. House GOP fanatics demanded that the FBI investigate Hillary's alleged false statements to Congress.

House GOP fanatics demanded that the FBI turn over the field agent's notes of the Hillary email interview, so rabid House Members could search for a prosecutable offense hiding in plain sight. Inexplicably, the FBI agreed to deliver the interview notes to the House. The animus of GOP House Members to bring down Hillary in 2016 is exceeded only by the mania shown by local and state officials in the *Salem Witch Trials* in 1692.

After FBI Director Comey announced there would be no recommendation to prosecute Hillary, Jason Chaffetz (R-UT), Chair, House Oversight and Government Reform Committee, invited Comey to explain his decision at a public hearing. Disappointed that the FBI would not recommend prosecution, Chaffetz asked Comey to investigate whether Hillary lied to Congress.

Comey explained that the FBI would need a Referral, which is a formal request. Chaffetz promised, *"You will have one in a few hours"*. Chaffetz and the other GOP Tea Party Members of Congress are bringing disrespect to the House and to the principles of American Government.

Separation of Powers is a bulwark of American Freedom. The Legislative Branch enacts laws. The

Executive Branch prosecutes criminal offenses. The Judicial Branch presides over trials of alleged offenses. GOP fanatics in the House want to force a criminal prosecution of Hillary to prevent her election as President. There is no doubt but that GOP fanatics in the House will urge impeachment of President Hillary Clinton on grounds of High Crimes and Misdemeanors.

There is also no doubt but that the Senate will acquit, if the Impeachment is made on political grounds. Under our Constitution, the American People hold federal government officials on a short leash. Every two years the entire House is up for election, together with one-third of the Senate. If the American People leave the Congress in the hands of fanatics under the influence of Breitbart News, the American People will have only themselves to blame.

Chapter 4.
Why We Cannot Allow Trump To Be President Trump

It is one thing if Trump is Trump in Trump Tower, in a Trump Hotel, or on a Trump Golf Course. Trump, as a private entrepreneur, can surf the internet at midnight, fill up on *Breitbart News From the Dark Side*, and send out tweets to disrupt, startle, and amaze the establishment. It is quite another thing if Trump is Trump at 1600 Pennsylvania Avenue. We cannot risk having an eccentric billionaire in the White House.

There is too much risk that President Trump might shoot his mouth off, commit a provocation, or overreact to exigent circumstances. The United States has the capability of blowing up the world several times over. Donald Trump has shown that he has a very short fuse. He has shown that he is very thin-skinned. He has shown that he cannot take criticism, and that he will not take direction from advisors.

Andrew Breitbart founded Breitbart News as a website. He researched hot button issues for Matthew Drudge of the Drudge report. He helped Arianna Huffington launch the Huffington Post, during Arianna's conservative days. He managed a video blog that depicted Department of Agriculture's Shirley Sherrod, an African American, discriminating against a white farmer. Breitbart & Co edited the video to give a false impression of Sherrod.

At age 43, Breitbart died in 2012 of a heart attack. Sherrod settled her defamation suit with Breitbart's Estate. Breitbart participated in the outing of Congressman Anthony Weiner for emailing naked photos of himself, and the undercover videos exposing fraudulent voter registration tactics of ACORN. After Breitbart's death, conspiracy theorists went into orbit. One rumor fantasied that Breitbart was about to release a video showing Barack Obama as a young man in the company of a couple of Weather Underground terrorists.

In real life, the GOP tried to smear Barack Obama in 2008 for associations with Bill Ayers, founder of Weather Underground Terrorists. The government prosecuted Ayers for 1968-1971 bombings protesting the Viet Nam War and the Pentagon. Ayer's conviction reversed on technical grounds because prosecutors suppressed evidence.

Ayers became a law-abiding citizen, and, after rehabilitation, served on two education related boards in Chicago. Obama also served on two boards with Ayers, and attended a fund-raiser where Ayers was present. When Ayers was a terrorist, Obama was eleven years of age. Obama had no connection with the Weather Underground Terrorists.

Trump began his 2015-16 Campaign with Corey Lewandowski as manager. Corey's motto was *'Let Trump be Trump'*. Trump easily won the GOP primaries, with the notable exception of Wisconsin where Ted Cruz took 48%, Trump, 35%, and Kasich, 14%. Trump won the GOP primaries without making prepared speeches or using Teleprompters.

Trump spoke extemporaneously, and said whatever came into his head. The GOP Base loved it. The Base consists of the Lowest Common Denominator, and can never vote a candidate into office in a General Election. Political professionals expected Trump to pivot toward a strategy that would appeal to a broader, General Electorate.

Paul Manafort was on the Trump Campaign Team as an advisor. Manafort does not have the most appealing public image. He advised dictator, Ferdinand Marcos, in the Philippines, and Viktor Yanukovych, Putin's pick for President of Ukraine in 2010. The People of Ukraine toppled Yanukovych in 2014. Manafort has the confidence of the GOP Establishment. Manafort favors a campaign style that is more traditional than *let Trump be Trump*.

When the polls started to fall, the Trump children and spouses began to lobby against the wild campaign style of Corey Lewandowski. Trump fired Corey and placed Manafort in charge. Trump was uncomfortable in the role of a conventional politician. Trump and Manafort decided to end their relationship after questions arose about off the book payments to Manafort in Ukraine.

Manafort's departure from the Campaign may relieve the scrutiny Trump receives for his phony bromance with Putin. Trump brought in Kellyanne Conway, of the Polling Company, and Stephen Bannon, Chair of Breitbart News, to head up the Campaign. Conway will remake Trump's image for the women of America. Bannon will continue spewing ideas from *Breitbart News and Views from the Dark Side*.

Republicans swear that they hate Hillary Clinton more than evil incarnate. Despite protestations to the contrary, it is nothing personal. Republicans hate whoever the Democrats' nominee is, because that person could keep the Republicans from the White House and the lucrative benefits of incumbency.

Remember when Howard Dean was the leading Democratic candidate in 2004. The Republican smear machine cast Dean as the biggest threat to the Republic. When Dean faded, John Kerry became the standard-bearer. The GOP dropped Dean as though he never existed. Republicans feared Kerry, because Kerry was a Navy hero of the Viet Nam War.

The GOP Liars Brigade maliciously shredded Kerry's War record. Enterprising, unprincipled Republicans procured affidavits from U.S. Navy personnel falsely attesting to Kerry's failure as an officer commanding a Swift Boat on the Mekong River. John O'Neil and Jerome Corsi, almost on cue, authored *"Unfit to Command"*. Kerry felt no obligation to rebut the GOP character attacks, and Bush prevailed. The GOP attack and smear against John Kerry brought a new word into the lexicon: *"Swiftboating"*.

Jerome Corsi later brought forth *The Obama Nation*, which the crazies heard as *The Abomination*. Corsi also published *Where's the Birth Certificate?* Corsi claims that President Obama wears a ring inscribed with the Shahada: *There is no God But Allah*. If the GOP crazies will pay for Corsi's output of trash, can we blame him for trying to make a buck?

Chapter 5.
Trump's Major Lies

I care about you. - to African Americans.

I care about you. - to Republicans.

I care about you. - to the American People.

Mexico is not sending us their best.

Mexico is sending us rapists.

I will make Mexico pay for the border wall.

President Obama was not born in the United States.

I am sending investigators to Hawaii to show Obama's birth certificate is a forgery.

I know more about ISIS than the generals.

After 9/11/01, I saw a video of New Jersey Moslems celebrating the attack.

I will never lie to you. - to the American People

Trump University has an "A" rating from the Better Business Bureau.

After four years, I guarantee you I will get 95% of the African American vote.

Trump hand-picked many of the instructors at Trump University.

Judge Curiel is biased toward Plaintiffs in the Trump University lawsuit.

I do not know anything about David Duke.

I have a relationship with Vladimir Putin.

Competitive bidding on price can save $300 billion on U.S. Prescription Drugs.

Trump questioned involvement of Ted Cruz's father with Lee Harvey Oswald and the assassination of President Kennedy.

No group has been damaged as much by Hillary Clinton's policies as African Americans.

I will deport 11 million undocumented immigrants.

I am not flip flopping on immigration policy.

I will win the 2016 election in a landslide.

If I lose, it will be because the election is rigged.

The only way I can lose Pennsylvania, is if people in some part of the state (Philadelphia) cheat.

I can stand in the middle of 5th Ave, shoot someone, and not lose a vote!?

Trump has lied so much that he feels free to put together support from groups that are adverse to each other. This is the same strategy employed by George W. Bush in 2000. Bush ran as a Compassionate Conservative. The Republican Base knew and liked Bush as a tough, swaggering conservative. Bush had their vote. Bush needed to build on the GOP Base Vote by adding votes of Women, Minorities, Blacks, and Hispanics.

By packaging Bush in a *Compassionate Conservative Wrapper*, GOP marketing pros improved Bush's poll numbers. The strategy was not entirely successful, because Al Gore beat Bush by 538,000 votes. The distribution of the Bush popular vote among the states allowed Bush to win a bare majority of 270 in the Electoral College.

It did not hurt Bush's chances in 2000 to have brother Jeb as Governor of Florida and Florida Secretary of State, Katherine Harris, as Co-Chair of the Bush Florida Campaign, to certify Bush's win in Florida by 537 votes.

Trump is trying the same tactic in 2016. Trump won the GOP Primaries by being Trump. Trump insulted and bullied everyone who opposed him. Trump announced a Moslem Ban to excite his base. As the General Election neared, Trump dropped the outright ban on Moslems. Trump switched to the dog whistle of *Extreme Vetting* of immigrants from war torn areas, which Christian

Nationalists will hear as a ban on Moslems. Constitutionalists will have to admit that *Extreme Vetting* passes muster.

Thus, Trump wins the support of the Nationalists and the Constitutionalists. Trump knows that most of his Base in the South and South West are lukewarm to the economic plight of African Americans. Trump announced that he is the champion of African Americans.

The GOP Base does not take such pledge to heart. Trump's rally audiences are mostly white. Trump could double his support in the Black Community by increasing his support from 1% to 2%. Kellyanne Conway will try to present Trump as a Gentleman and friend of women. Trump has already said that nothing matters so long as you have a good piece.

Trump casts himself as a disrupter of the *status quo*. To win, he must show that the future of America is bleak unless Trump wins. He must continue to set group against group, and threaten that there will be civil unrest without Trump's brand of law and order. Stephen Bannon of *Breitbart News* has the task of stirring up racial discontent and class dissension, so that only Trump can save the nation. Trump endeavors to turn Blacks against Hispanics and Moslems, by blaming immigrants for taking jobs from African Americans.

Trump cannot win on policy issues, because he has no intelligible policies. His overarching message is that America is broken. He claims, *"I alone can fix it"*. To boost his cratered campaign, he must attack Hillary Clinton personally. Trump claims that Hillary is not healthy enough to serve as President.

Stephen Bannon and *Breitbart News from the Dark Side* no doubt will fan the rumors of Hillary's health. Rudy

Giuliani makes special appearances on cable TV to raise doubts about Hillary's health. Giuliani backed out of a campaign against Hillary when she ran for the Senate in New York, a prize that Rudy fancied.

The reason Rudy could not take on Hillary was poor health. Rudy's, not Hillary's. Rudy is pathetic as he tried to glom on to Chris Christie, and then to Trump. Rudy tries to sell security services based on his serving as Mayor on 9/11, and, if he can connect with a GOP President, Rudy can sell more security services. Rudy is the poster boy for why the GOP has no soul. Too many greedy opportunists chasing money. Pathetic.

Chapter 6.
The Problem with Trade Agreements

Ross Perot highlighted the issue in 1992. *'That giant sucking sound will be American jobs going over the border to Mexico.'* Bill Clinton beat Perot and Poppy Bush with less than forty percent of the popular vote. Clinton went on to sign NAFTA, the *North American Free Trade Agreement*. The *Maquiladora Industry* sprang up on the Mexican side of the U.S. Border. Manufacturers shipped components to Tijuana or Juarez.

Mexicans assembled the components, and the Companies shipped the finished product to the U.S. for sale with no or low tariffs. NAFTA also allowed sale in the U.S. of automobiles manufactured in Mexico. The U.S. signed a series of trade agreements that made the U.S. market wide open for foreign exploitation.

Manufacturers search for low-wage-rate countries in a race to the bottom. The result is the U.S. rust belt from Pennsylvania to Wisconsin. TPP, *Trans-Pacific Partnership*, is the hot button issue for 2016-17.

President Obama supports TPP, Hillary dropped her support after Bernie Sanders campaigned against it in the Democratic Primary. Obama argues that the U.S. must join TPP, or allow China and other countries to write the rules. The devil of course is in the details. The TPP is not the problem. It is the provisions in the TPP. The U.S. starts with a major trade handicap. The U.S. worker may be paid $18.00 an hour. A worker in Viet Nam may be paid $ 0.50 an hour. American products cannot compete on price.

America focuses on trade agreement provisions that govern working conditions and prohibitions on excluded categories, such as goods produced by child labor or convict labor. The U.S. seeks to impose OSHA requirements on foreign manufacturers—possibly with the idea that if overheads go up in China—it will make the U.S. more competitive.

TPP is supposed to remove or lower tariffs substantially for all countries. Tariffs and quotas, however, are the best way to equalize trade. America has been on a manufacturing slide for over fifty years. The first exports from Japan in the late 1940s were tinny toys that were laughable. When Sony started after World War II, there were Japanese workers primitively laying out yards of recording tape on factory floors to be hand brushed with magnetic coating.

In 1950, the Korean War diverted American Industry back to war manufacturing. This allowed the Japanese to crack the U.S. automobile market. Toyota and Datsun started shipping cars to America. By the 1970s, American consumers noted that Toyota Corollas could clock 200,000 miles. All of the American consumer electronic inventions migrated to Japan for manufacture. No one was laughing at Japanese products any more.

As wages rose in Japan, work migrated to Korea. In the 1980s, made in Korea was the label on U.S. clothing. Korean car makers Hyundai and KIA later became household terms. As Korean wages rose, some work exported to China and India. The U.S. cannot continue to run a trade deficit with the major exporting countries. The U.S. cannot approve a trade agreement just because it bans child labor or prison made products, or forces American working conditions on foreign countries.

At the end of the day, the U.S must have provisions in every trade agreement that allow tariffs or quotas or ways to counter currency manipulation to protect American manufacture. This, of course, is the gist of the problem. The idea of free trade is to eliminate quotas and balancing tariffs. U.S. Trade Deficits of $400 billion a year are not sustainable.

The race to the bottom rages within U.S. borders as well. U.S carmakers were paying labor $38.00 an hour. After the General Motors bankruptcy, the wage reduced to $18.00 an hour for new employees. Carmakers struggle with burgeoning medical care and pension costs taken on in the course of negotiating union contracts.

Instead of working with the Obama Administration to improve the *Affordable Care Act* (ACA), Republicans adopted a scorched earth policy to scuttle ACA. The Act passed a Democrat controlled Congress in 2010. Republicans vowed to *Repeal and Replace* ACA.

Six years later, there is no GOP health care plan. After a few years, the cry was to Repeal, but not to Replace. A few GOP stalwarts came up with ACA Light, which contained ACA's popular features such as allowing children on parents' policies until age 26, and banning exclusion because of preexisting medical condition.

Republicans in general sabotaged universal health care even though it was a GOP idea. The main reason for GOP opposition is to make sure Obama does not receive credit for anything in his term in office. If anyone wants a gold plated, single payer, health care plan, get elected to Congress.

Donald Trump is no better than the scorched earth Republicans in Congress. Trump knows nothing about universal health care. He opposes ACA because it thrills the GOP Base. Republicans are so crazy in their opposition to ACA that the House passed bills to repeal or cripple ACA *fifty times*.

When new GOP Members elected to the House in 2012 or 2014, it was a rite of passage for each newbie to sponsor yet one more repeal of ACA, despite the dozens of repeal bills previously passed by a rabid GOP House. The newbie then had Tea Party credentials, even if the newbie knew nothing about universal health care.

Chapter 7.
Trump's Motivations Remain a Puzzle

Why would a millionaire give up a cozy life ensconced in the luxury of Trump Tower, only to risk humiliation on the hustings or life in a goldfish bowl? The answer is ego needs. Trump's overwhelming ego may need new worlds to conquer. Or, he needs stroking by the Nation to overcome the abandonment and rejection complex that arose when Fred Trump sent his incorrigible 15 year old son to Military School in a failed attempt to instill discipline. Donald has been toying with the idea of running for President for several election cycles.

Trump was not sure if he was a Democrat or a Republican. Looking ahead to 2016, Trump decided to run as a Republican. That decision alone cast Trump as an advocate who wanted to *Make America Great Again.* Republicans agreed with Trump that there should be no recognition of Barack Obama's success after taking the helm during the worst recession since the great depression.

When the U.S. auto industry teetered on insolvency, Obama pushed through a financial aid package that saved General Motors and Fiat Chrysler. Republicans wanted to allow market forces to clear out weaker companies. What is not so widely known is that Obama's financial aid to the auto industry likely saved the Ford Motor Company as well.

Ford was not insolvent. Ford, however, relied upon many of the parts manufacturers that also supplied GM and Chrysler. If GM and Chrysler failed, the parts manufacturers would fail. Ford could not survive as a stand alone island, if the rest of the U.S. auto industry failed.

Once Trump decided to run in the 2016 cycle, he could not resist the temptation to campaign for the *Archie Bunker* vote. Ronald Reagan wrote the script by beating Jimmy Carter in 1980 with a large number of Reagan (Blue Collar) Democrats. Thirty-six years later, changing demographics made it mandatory for Trump to carve out a constituency of Blue Collar Democrats. Otherwise, the voting numbers do not add up for Republicans.

This time-tested Republican strategy requires the GOP candidate to gin up wedge issues to divide the once dominate white voters from the growing number of minority voters.

The social issues provide the wedges used to divide and conquer. Trump does not really care about wedge issues. The only issue the Trump Team fretted over at the 2016 Convention in Cleveland was Trump's concerted effort to remove the Platform Plank that supported a strong NATO. President Putin approved. Tony Perkins, of *Family Research Council* fame, worked out most of the wedge issues on abortion, gays, and the God-given right of bakers, florists, and ministers, to refuse to cater to gay marriages.

The most recent hot-button, GOP, wedge issue is the legislation aimed at making sure that only those born female can use female bathrooms. At first blush, the birth bathroom issue seems to be as nonsensical as the birther campaign against Obama. Ask any mother in Athens, Georgia, however, if she could tolerate a former man in her daughter's bathroom—and she will scream, *"Heavens No!"*

Think about it. If Caitland Jenner enters a bathroom to go to the toilet, would that harm the other females present? The fact that Caitland was born Bruce is not controlling. GOP wedge issue panderers will argue that there are men roaming the streets, looking for ways to enter Ladies Rooms. Trans-gender folks, who end up as females, have nowhere else to go. The U.S. Supreme Court will rule on the issue by June 2017.

Trump carefully laid out his plan to run for President as a Republican. It has been a few years since Trump jumped on the birther bandwagon to try to delegitimize Obama, and, in fact, became Birther in Chief. Trump knew President Obama was born in Hawaii. Trump wanted to discredit Obama's presidency.

Trump understood that—if he ran as a Republican—there would be a crazy Right Wing, which would believe any smear against a Democratic President. *There have always been crazies in the GOP*, long before the John Birch Society. Joseph Welch at one time thought that Dwight Eisenhower and his brother Milton were communist dupes.

Trump claimed that he sent investigators to Hawaii to out the ruse by Obama's mother, who cleverly paid for an ad in the Hawaii newspaper to stage an American birth that would enable her son to run for president decades later.

Those who view Trump only as a stream of present consciousness are mistaken. Trump plans his moves far in advance. Trump initiated his birther gambit against President Obama years in advance of his campaign for President. Few understood what Donald had in mind as he became *Birther in Chief* in 2011. An effective way to defeat Hillary is to escalate the GOP effort to delegitimize President Obama.

Trump's engagement of Paul Manafort was a well-thought-out opening to appease Vladimir Putin, as is Trump's nonchalant attitude toward Russian aggression in Ukraine. Trump's campaign to win the *Archie Bunker* vote is not a spontaneous blurting out of minority-bashing words in the heat of a campaign rally Trump planned his subversion of Judge Curiel's impartiality well in advance of his outburst.

The attack on the judiciary fit well with his insult to Mexico. The saga of the wall may well have been more to try to force dismissal of the lawsuit against Trump University than to rally *Archie Bunker* to the Trump cause.

Hillary may be mistaken when she claims that Trump is *"Dangerously Incoherent"*. Trump may be more hazardous as *"Dangerously Coherent"*. Trump may be confused about the possibility of winning the Presidency with an *Archie Bunker* campaign. Trump, however, is clear that he wants to be a disruptor, that he wants to stir up resentment with wedge issues, and that he sees a path to victory only by winning over Reagan's *Blue Collar Democrats*.

Trump's arrogance ultimately will sink his campaign. He brags that he knows more about ISIS than the Generals in the field do. His proposed income tax rates are a give-away to himself and the upper one percent. His proposed abolishment of the inheritance tax is nothing more than a short cut to the self-serving objectives of the Trump Family Trust. His greatest mistake is treating the electorate as fools.

Things went swimmingly well during the Primaries. Trump entertained the audiences at spirited GOP rallies. His sixteen opponents melted away. After winning most of the primaries, however, he did not pivot to a General Election Strategy. He feels that fifteen thousand cheering supporters at General Election rallies count for as much as the supporters during the primaries. For every cheering supporter at his General Election rallies, however, there are thousands of voters, who have had enough of Donald Trump and his faux *Archie Bunker* mentality.

Virtual Reality

As producer of the TV show, *The Apprentice*, Donald Trump controlled the script. He was always the hero. He never lost. He fired other people. No one could lay a glove on him. He desperately seeks to control the script of the 2016 presidential election cycle. As the hero in his real life election campaign show, he cannot play the part of a loser. During the primaries, he wrote the script. The crowds at the rallies played their part perfectly, and cheered their hero as he bashed immigrants, Mexicans, Moslems, and Minorities.

Even his opponents played their part by dropping out of the race, almost on cue. The polls saluted him as a winner. The media were favorably impressed. He benefitted from the contest between Hillary Clinton and Bernie Sanders. He tried to drive a wedge between the two progressive candidates by sympathizing with the apparent favoritism shown to the long-time Democrat by the Democratic National Committee.

Inexplicable, he could not accept victory at the end of his triumph in the primaries. He refused to pivot to a General Election Campaign. He knew more than the political experts. He knew he could win by playing to the *Archie Bunker* vote. The Republican Convention was disappointing. A Mixed Martial Arts business owner, then Pat Smith agonizing over loss of her son, Sean, in the terrorist attack on the American Mission at Benghazi, Chris Christie with a mock indictment of Hillary, Rudy Giuliani with a rabid mock prosecution of Hillary, and the Trump children, trying to humanize the Patrón.

The Pivot

Trump does not want to pivot because he thinks that would be dishonest. So he will just keep telling the same old lies. He appeared at a rally in West Bend, Wisconsin, forty miles northwest of the riots in Milwaukee over the shooting by a black police officer of an armed black man fleeing a traffic stop. The camera at the Trump rally showed only Trump, and not the audience. Trump suddenly became the champion of the underclass of impoverished African-Americans. West Bend is less than one percent black.

Trump's cheering audience sounded more like *Archie Bunker* than *The Jeffersons*. Trump paid lip service to the needs of the black community, but Trump declined to speak at the NAACP, the Urban League, or the Convention of Black and Hispanic Journalists. Trump's support in the Black Community is at an historic low of 1%. The West Bend speech will not improve the numbers because the speech obviously was for show.

Whether a pivot or a pirouette, Trump is showing some fancy footwork. On June 20, 2016, Trump fired Corey Lewandowski as Campaign Manager. Corey's offense was allowing Trump to be Trump. What worked wonders during the primaries was wreaking havoc in the General Election Campaign. Trump brought in Paul Manafort as Campaign Manager. Conventional wisdom concluded that with an adult at the top, the childish outbursts would end.

Manafort did not travel with the candidate. Trump knew from plummeting poll numbers that he risked losing badly on November 8, 2016. Trump's ego cannot accept that he would bear responsibility for losing the election. In Pennsylvania the previous day, Trump stated that the only way he could lose was if people in some parts of the state would cheat by voting multiple times for his opponent.

The cheaters of course would be urban dwellers and minorities, especially in Philadelphia. Trump also made it clear that he was fighting the *"crooked media"*, who were distorting the news. There would be external reasons for his loss, not his fault.

There was a major pivot on August 16. Trump promoted advisor Kellyanne Conway as Campaign Trip Manager. Conway will travel with Trump, ostensibly to keep Trump from speaking Trump-Talk, or at least to explain to the candidate the reasons for fluctuations in daily polls. Conway is CEO of The Polling Company. Conway has to explain the complexities of the internals of polls.

If you attack a Gold Star parent, who lost a child in the military service of the Nation, your poll numbers likely will go down. If you question the impartiality of an American-born judge, because of his Mexican ancestry, your poll numbers will go down (even if you are building a wall to keep Mexicans and immigrants from Central America from using the Mexican Border to cross illegally into the U.S.).

Trump also brought in heavyweight Stephen Bannon as Campaign CEO, presumably to gin up an October surprise to swamp the Hillary Clinton Campaign Boat. Bannon is a co-founder of the Breitbart website. Breitbart is Fox News on steroids. Breitbart will concoct and disseminate stories about Bill Clinton's escapades, present and past. Hillary faced Bill stories since the 1980s.

It will be Bannon's job to make Hillary the villain. Breitbart will spread conspiracy theories about the Clinton Foundation, the State Department, and pay for play politics. Bannon's answer to Trump's low poll numbers will be, *'We've got a remedy for whatever Ailes you.'*

Roger Ailes, recently separated from Fox News after sexual harassment allegations, will unofficially advise Trump on how to beat Hillary. Ailes helped Poppy Bush overcome Mike Dukakis' 17 point lead coming out of the Democratic Convention in 1988. At the top of this sludge heap, Paul Manafort continued temporarily to reign as overall Campaign Chair.

It is ironic that Donald Segretti went to jail for minor shenanigans committed while working for Dwight Chapin, Nixon's CEO of Dirty Tricks. Today, opposition research can openly use fabricated stories to destroy someone's character and reputation, and escape punishment. Libel laws are little help to public figures.

It is also ironic that George W. Bush's Brain, Karl Rove, who cut his teeth as an assistant to Donald Segretti in the early 70s, escaped prosecution for his role in outing Valerie Plame as a covert CIA agent. Rove, Bush's Assistant Chief of Staff, and Scooter Libby, Dick Cheney's Chief of Staff, were tasked by Cheney to discredit

Ambassador Joseph Wilson, who debunked the Bush-Cheney fable that Saddam Hussein bought yellowcake uranium from Niger. Wilson was married to Plame.

Bush, Cheney, Rumsfeld, Condi Rice, and Paul Wolfowitz waged a campaign of disinformation to hoodwink the American People into supporting the Neocons and the Religious Right in the 2003 invasion of Iraq. The Bush Party Line was that the Iraq invasion was necessary to eliminate Saddam's Weapons of Mass Destruction (WMD). The Party Mantra, incanted daily by the Bush Team to condition the American People for War, was, *'We do not want the first sign of WMD to be a mushroom cloud.'*

Ambassador Wilson rebutted the nuclear aspect of alleged WMD in Iraq. Wilson wrote an Op-Ed in the New York Times on July 6, 2003. *"What I Didn't Find in Africa"*. Cheney was furious. Scooter Libby and Karl Rove were turned loose to discredit Wilson. Various members of the Bush team disclosed that Valerie Plame was a covert CIA operative. The clumsy idea of the Bush Team was that Valerie Plame sent Wilson to Niger, not the CIA.

Scooter Libby was indicted, convicted, and sentenced to prison and fined. Karl Rove testified before the Grand Jury *five* times. Rove admitted his involvement, but denied that he knew of Plame's status as a covert CIA Agent. Scooter Libby was convicted for telling the truth. Karl Rove was never indicted because Rove knew how to lie convincingly. Rove, who forms a bridge from the Dirty Tricks era of Nixon to the GOP campaign sleaze of today, went on to handle hundreds of millions of dollars as CEO of tax exempt organizations, *American Crossroads* and *Crossroads GPS*. Bush commuted Libby's prison sentence. Cheney wanted a pardon for Libby.

Chapter 8.
Electoral College Math

Theoretically, Trump could win with the eleven largest states' electoral votes: California (55), Texas (38), New York (29), Florida (29), Illinois (20), Pennsylvania (20), Ohio (18), Michigan and Georgia (16), North Carolina (15), and New Jersey (14). Since California, New York, and Illinois are heavily Blue states, Trump will need to replace those Electoral Votes with Virginia (13), Arizona and Tennessee (11), Missouri (10), Alabama, South Carolina, and Colorado (9), Louisiana and Kentucky (8) and Iowa, Kansas, Oklahoma, Nevada , and Mississippi (6), Nebraska and New Mexico (5), New Hampshire and Idaho (4), and Alaska, North Dakota, Montana, and Wyoming (3).

States Trump Needs In 2016

Texas	(38)
Florida	(29)
Pennsylvania	(20)
Ohio	(18)
Michigan, Georgia x 16	(32)
North Carolina	(15)
Virginia	(13)
Arizona, Tennessee x 11	(22)
Missouri	(10)
Alabama, Colorado, S Carolina x 9	(27)
Kentucky, Louisiana x 8	(16)
Kansas, Oklahoma, Mississippi x 6	(18)
Nebraska, New Mexico x 5	(10)
Idaho	(04)
AK, N Dakota, Montana, Wyoming x 3	(12)

Total 284

If Trump took all of the above states, but lost Virginia (13), Trump would win with 271 Electoral Votes.

However, if Trump lost even one of Florida, Pennsylvania, Ohio, or Michigan, his numbers fall short of 270. At the end of the day on 11/8/16, the future of America will depend on vote tallies in New Hampshire, Virginia, Colorado, Nevada, and New Mexico. States with less than five percent of the population likely will determine the outcome of the election for a Nation of 350,000,000.

There will be trends and countertrends that influence vote totals. Gary Johnson, former Governor of New Mexico, heads the Libertarian Party. Johnson, in favor of smaller government, may draw more from both parties. In New Mexico, the tally could be Clinton 45%, Trump 42, Johnson 12%, Stein 1. The Hispanic vote in Florida, New Jersey, Arizona, California, Colorado, New Mexico, and Texas, may punish Trump for proposing to build a wall and for hate speech. The Moslem vote in Ohio and Michigan may turn against Trump for his proposed Moslem ban. Trump may resort to Realpolitik, promising jobs and fair play to leaders of disaffected communities in exchange for endorsement.

The polls taken in June are meaningless. When 57% of women say they will never vote for Trump, they are merely saying that they view many of Trump's statements in May and June as offensive. That is a cerebral response to a question posed more or less to their intellects. It was politically correct for the media, party leaders, and the electorate, to be against Trump in June.

On November 8, 2016, the women and the men will vote their gut and their heart. The result on Election Day will depend more on what they feel rather than on what they think. Everyone has reservations about the *Nanny State*.

Everyone regrets America's loss of jobs and manufacturing capacity. Everyone is concerned about National Defense and Security. Voters have anxieties about our military involvement in Afghanistan, Iraq, and Syria. There are concerns about our failure to stop the chaos, death and displacement of population in Syria. Many voters feel threatened by wholesale immigration, particularly from disrupted areas without opportunity for proper vetting of who exactly is coming to America.

Voters view Trump as a disruptor of the status quo. Whoever is dissatisfied—with big government, the economy, loss of jobs and manufacturing capability, deteriorating international relations, chaos in the Middle East, stresses on the Middle Class, falling standard of living, poorly regulated immigration, terrorism, or whatever—will look to Trump for change.

Trump could win the presidency, while the Democrats take control of the Senate. Wisconsinites may decide that Russ Feingold should have his job back from Ron Johnson. Republicans could easily lose another half dozen Senate races in 2016. Even John McCain is running scared.

For those looking for a blowout route by the Democrats in 2016, we point to 2000, where the level of frustration and dissatisfaction was less than in 2016. George W. Bush won by a majority of one electoral vote, with 271. Gore garnered 538,000 more popular votes than Bush. If New Hampshire (or any other state had flipped to the Democrats), Al Gore would have been elected President.

The U.S. Supreme Court stopped the vote recount in Florida in a Right Wing decision made possible by Chief Justice William H. Rehnquist. Bush just happened to have his brother Jeb as Governor of Florida and his campaign co-chair, Katherine Harris, as Florida Secretary of State, who, despite the inherent conflict of interest, certified Bush the winner.

The 2008 election, between Barack Obama and John McCain, was about hope and change. Most Americans wanted to end the wars in Afghanistan and Iraq. Obama took 365 electoral votes to McCain's 173. The economy fell apart in the summer of 2008. Lehman Brother, who had been around since the 1850s, filed for bankruptcy protection on September 15, 2008, the effective date Senator McCain lost the 2008 election. The day of the filing, Lehman Brother had assets of more than $600 billion U.S. Dollars.

It is a stark reminder of the total collapse of the credit markets in the U.S. and around the world in 2008 that Lehman Brothers was unable to borrow a few hundred million to provide operating liquidity to secure their assets of $600 billion. John McCain never had a chance to win after the financial collapse of the summer and fall of 2008. He is still bitter about the loss that fate and the Junior Senator from Illinois handed him.

New York as Keystone State in 2016?

Pennsylvania used to be key to victory in the Electoral College. Then, there is the interesting fact that the Republicans never won the Presidency without winning Ohio. In 2016, the key for the GOP might be New York. If Trump writes off Electoral Votes of California (55), New York (29), and Illinois (20), as too blue to contest, it takes a whole basket full of states to make up the deficit of 104 votes.

Why should Trump, the quintessential New Yorker, give up on his home state? Up-state New York tends to vote Republican. The City cancels out the Up-state vote to put the state in the Democrats' corner. Trump has his headquarters in New York City. Trump Tower dominates Fifth Avenue. Look at what happens if Trump takes New York.

The loss of any one of Florida (29), or Pennsylvania (20), or Ohio (18), or Michigan (16), alone, would not be fatal. Listen carefully to election results on the evening of November 8, 2016. If Trump takes New York, there will be no landslide for the Democrats. If Trump also takes Florida or Pennsylvania, and either Ohio or Michigan, the GOP likely will prevail.

John Kasich, Governor of Ohio, could help keep the Midwest Republican. Former House Speaker Newt Gingrich has national name recognition, and initially supported trump. Gingrich turned to criticizing Trump in June, however. Governor Kasich seems to be aloof in supporting Trump. New Mexico Governor, Susanna Martinez, would help with Hispanics, but is a doubtful choice after boycotting a Trump rally in Albuquerque in June. Raoul Labrador (R-UT) would also help with Hispanics.

Cruz Control

To control the GOP Convention, Trump had to wrest power away from Ted Cruz, who, as of June, had (1) more campaign money in the bank than Trump, and (2) a majority of pledged delegates on the Convention Rules Committee. The Rules Committee met a week before the Convention to decide whether Pledged Delegates should be free to vote their consciences on the first ballot. Releasing the Delegates from their Pledge is part of a scenario for the rescue of the GOP by a White Knight.

The problem is that there are few rescuers with stature, Mitt Romney comes to mind. The reaction on the

Convention Floor to Romney likely would be, 'Been There, Done That', twice. That leaves Ted Cruz to offer himself as Standard Bearer instead of Trump. Evangelicals favor Cruz. Conservatives support him. Tea Party fanatics adore him. One minor problem. Party Leaders cannot abide Cruz. Mitch McConnell would not lift a finger to help Cruz. Neither would Speaker Ryan.

Former Speaker John Boehner openly curses Cruz. Cruz prides himself on running against the Washington Establishment. In 2013, Cruz and Senator Mike Lee (R-UT) advocated a government shutdown, if necessary, to defund the *Affordable Care Act*. Cruz and Lee paralyzed the Senate. Cruz crossed over to the House side to lobby House Tea Party Members to choose government shutdown as the alternative to funding Affordable Care. Speaker Boehner fumed over Cruz acting as House Whip in opposition to the Speaker.

The Tea Party thought shutting down the government was a great idea. That is why many of them came to Washington. Without budget authorization, the government shut down for 19 days. Eighty percent of the American People thought the Shutdown was a bad idea, and blamed Republicans. Speaker Boehner decided to retire. No one in GOP Leadership would have supported a Cruz revolt at the 2016 Convention.

Cruz addressed the delegated at the GOP 2016 Convention. Everyone expected him to endorse Donald Trump. Cruz reached the end of his speech. The delegates sat on the edge of their seats. Cruz finally advised, *'Vote your conscience.'* The delegates booed Cruz off the stage. At first, everyone thought that Cruz lost favor. As the Trump Campaign continued to unfold as a Train Wreck,

Cruz's decision not to endorse Trump looks better every day.

Electors Follow Population

Power in the Electoral College follows the population shift to the South and West. In 1860, New York had 35 Electoral Votes. California and Texas had 4 each. Florida had 3. Pennsylvania had 27 Electors, Ohio 23. In 1960, New York had 45 Electors, California and Pennsylvania 32, Texas 24, Ohio 25, and Florida 10. In 2016, California has 55 Electors, Texas 38, New York and Florida 29, Pennsylvania 20, and Ohio 18. Losing Ohio would not be fatal to the GOP in 2016.

If Gary Johnson and Evan McMullin win enough votes in New Mexico, Utah, and Idaho, the election could go to the House. Every State would have one vote. A GOP House likely would choose Donald Trump as President.

Chapter 9.
You Have Mail! [and it never goes away].

Republicans are hysterical in their opposition to Hillary Clinton. When excitement tapered off during the GOP Convention in July 2016, their rallying cry refocused the attention of the delegates. *'Lock her up. Lock her up!'* Chris Christie delighted the mob with a mock prosecution of HRC.

Hillary's alleged crimes are (1) failure to save the lives of Ambassador Chris Stevens and three other officials at the U.S. Diplomatic Mission and Annex in Benghazi, Libya, during a terrorist attack in 2012, (2) misuse of email while Secretary of State, and (3) conflict of interest with the Clinton Foundation while she was Secretary of State.

Nine Benghazi investigations generated more heat than light. According to House Majority Leader Kevin

McCarthy (R-CA), the GOP constituted one final Select Committee on Benghazi, under former prosecutor Trey Goudy (R-SC), to bring down Hillary's poll numbers. This admission cost McCarthy the Speaker's gavel. Paul Ryan stepped in to fill the void. After 11 hours of HRC testimony, Goudy was unable to find a smoking gun.

Benghazi, the U.S. mission in eastern Libya, was an accident waiting to happen. The facilities were nothing more than villas, which were not together and not protected by a perimeter wall. The annex was separate and apart from the diplomatic mission. The CIA controlled the annex, but HRC is not supposed to talk about that minor point. Another minor point, Congress cut funding from the State Department budget requested by the Obama Administration for improving security. Libya had no effective government in 2014. Gangs of militias and terror organizations roamed freely in Benghazi. The spark for the revolution against Moamar Ghaddafi burst into flame in Benghazi. Ambassador Chris Stevens and the CIA wanted to be in Benghazi because that is where the action was.

Susan Rice had the job of appearing on the Sunday talk shows to explain what happened in Benghazi. Rice read from talking points that blamed the Benghazi attack on the anti-Moslem video made by a Los Angeles, California, minister. Since the CIA controlled the Benghazi Annex, the CIA may have been involved in revising (and camouflaging) the talking points for Susan Rice to read. Or, the reference to the video may have been inserted by one of the wizards working clean-up in the White House.

The Obama Administration, which has a tendency to dress up bad news, should have announced that several trucks with terrorists attacked the Benghazi Diplomatic Mission with rocket-propelled grenades and automatic weapons—killing Ambassador Chris Stevens and three other officials—and that the matter is under investigation. Period. Full stop. Just for the record, there were riots in Cairo after the anti-Moslem video played in Egypt.

Republicans went crazy after Susan Rice's explanation for Benghazi. Rice had to withdraw her name from consideration as Secretary of State. Republicans falsely accused Hillary of murder. Pat Smith, mother of Sean Smith, verbally attacked Hillary at the GOP Convention. Republicans invented a scenario that never happened. Republicans fantasized that Hillary gave a stand down order to the Department of Defense to prevent relief of the Benghazi Mission under attack. Remember, it is not personal.

If Hillary withdrew from the presidential race, Republicans would move on to smear the next nominee of the Democrats. The only reason for republicans to invent the stand down order is to block Hillary's election as President. The only reason Republicans constituted the Select Committee on Benghazi under former prosecutor Trey Gowdy was to block Hillary's election.

Hillary made a strategic mistake when she took on the mantle of Secretary of State. As a former President with voluminous correspondence, Bill Clinton had an email server in the basement of the Clinton home in Chappaqua, New York. HRC also had voluminous personal correspondence that she did not want to broadcast via the State Department servers.

After seven years of investigation and rampant GOP criticism during White House years, both Clintons were gun shy about the confidentiality of their personal correspondence. Bill Clinton or one of the Clinton's aides should have negated the idea of using the home server for

State Department email. If the server is located at Foggy Bottom, security against hacking is a State Department problem. Using a home server puts hacking risk on the Clintons.

The issue of classifying documents in an appropriate manner is on HRC, wherever the server is located. Security Classification is at best a messy operation. Facts and descriptors are sometimes disseminated with no or low classification. Upon review, the Classification may be elevated to a higher level in retrospect. This may have happened to some of the HRC emails at State. Sometimes, simple words are pregnant with state sensitivity. The word *"drone"*, for example may raise problems in an unclassified email.

If the writer couples the word "drone" with the name of a country, *"Yemen"*, for example, the Classification may be headed toward *"Top Secret"*, depending on the context. Why is drone so touchy? Simple. The Executive Branch of the Government of the United States has ordered it so. It doesn't matter, except maybe at a criminal trial for security violation, that the secret information is wholly available from public sources such as newspapers, journals, and the internet.

The law protects the President and the Vice President, who may lawfully declassify secret information on the spot. The Secretary of State has no such protection. FBI Director James B. Comey announced that the FBI would not recommend prosecution of Hillary for mishandling emails at the State Department. Comey went on gratuitously to criticize Hillary for sloppiness in handling emails. This criticism was meant more to preserve Comey's reputation for character and validate his decision not to recommend prosecution than to provide meaningful analysis.

Comey should have laid out how many emails Hillary botched from a security perspective, and how she messed up. If it is all too hush, hush to talk about, maybe Director Comey should have said nothing more than that the FBI would not recommend prosecution.

Our Manchurian Candidate

Americans are intrigued and concerned about the bromance between Donald Trump, GOP nominee for president, and Vladimir Putin, President of the Russian Federation. Putin is surrounded in Europe by NATO allies and candidate states eager for admission to NATO. Putin yearns for the power and prestige of Russia and the Soviet Union of yesteryear. Trump seems to yearn for yesteryear as well. It is not clear whether Trump wants to turn the clock back to the 1960s when George Wallace started his many terms as Governor of Alabama, or to the mid-1950s when Orval Faubus began his term as Governor of Arkansas.

Putin objects that NATO is trying to enemies of Russia out of every European country on or near the Russian border. Russia swallowed Ukraine in 1783 under the leadership of Catherine the Great. Ukraine won independence in 1991, with the disintegration of the Soviet Union. Putin decided that Russian naval power needed Crimea, and so invaded in 2014. Russian troops, masquerading as volunteers, are waging war against eastern and southern Ukraine.

Putin wants to weaken NATO. Donald Trump has suggested that as President he would adopt policies that would tend to weaken NATO. From 2012-2014 Trump's Campaign Manager, Paul Manafort, advised Viktor Yanukovych, Premier of Ukraine, and a protégé of Putin's. There is a question of whether Manafort also represented

Yanukovych in the U.S., and whether Manfort should have registered with the Justice Department as a Foreign Agent. In February 2014, Ukraine ousted Yanukovych in a coup d'état. Trump's employment of Manafort can be viewed as Trump reaching out to Putin. Trump admires Putin's leadership. Putin opines favorably on Trump's wisdom.

The more Trump views NATO as an anachronism, the wiser Trump appears to Putin. On more than one occasion, Trump wistfully remarked that, Wouldn't it be nice if the U.S and Russia got along? To become Putin's BFF, all Trump has to do is sabotage NATO. This would free up Russia to engage in further expansion in Ukraine and the Baltic States. If Trump is elected President, Paul Manafort's business as a Foreign Agent will boom. If Hillary is elected, Manafort may be investigated. Manafort departed from the Trump Campaign during the shakeup that brought in Stephen Bannon and Kellyanne Conway as CEO and Manager, respectively, of the Campaign to let Trump be Trump but to make voters think that Trump is really someone much less frightening.

October Surprise

On October 28, 2016, FBI Director Comey dropped a bombshell. Additional emails have come to light. The FBI will review to determine if the new emails are pertinent to the investigation of Hillary's emails at State. Rumor has it that the investigation into Anthony Wiener's alleged texting with a minor female disclosed additional emails. Huma Abedin, Hillary's top confidant, apparently shared a laptop with Anthony Wiener. With only eleven days to Election Day, everyone is shouting at FBI Director Comey to disclose more details of what the FBI discovered.

No matter what FBI Director Coney does now, he will be in the middle of a constitutional crisis. Republicans want to jail Hillary to allow Trump to win. Democrats are outraged that the FBI could cause uncertainty eleven days before the election.

Chapter 10.
Implosion of the Let Trump be Trump Campaign

Trump started the 2016 Campaign Cycle as a TV personality. With or without a script, Trump energetically projected and promoted Trump. Obviously, it was more of a pure, unadulterated Trump when he did not have a script. Tea Party fanatics loved it. The anti-establishment Republican Base loved it. The Nationalists loved it. Trump promised to deport 11 million undocumented immigrants.

This made Mitt Romney's self-deportation scheme from 2008 look liberal. Trump promised to be humane. There would be no internment camps. Folks in the fever swamp led by Stephen Bannon and *Breitbart News from the Dark Side* loved it. There were two major structural problems. Trump had no policy. He was just shooting his mouth off. The other problem was that the Electoral College Vote Computer kept flashing red.

There was no path available for Trump to reach 270 Electoral Votes if Trump garnered 1% of the African American Vote and only 22% of the Hispanic Vote. The Trump Campaign went into a tailspin. By August 23, 2016, Trump acted out of desperation. He told African Americans. You have no job. You live in poverty. You are shot in the streets. The Democrats have run your cities for fifty years. *"What the hell do you have to lose?"*

Trump schedulers set Thursday, August 25, as the date for a major immigration speech in Colorado. The schedulers overlooked the obvious. Trump had no immigration policy to announce. Trump used deportation of

11 million illegals as red meat to excite his Base. He had just announced to Hispanic leaders, however, that he would not be that severe on deportation. Trump canceled the August 25 rally in Colorado.

Without an Immigration Policy, there could be no defining immigration speech. Immigration has dogged Republicans for years. GOP Nationalists want mass deportations. GOP realists cannot see 270 electoral votes without minority support. Marco Rubio stumbled on this problem in 2013. Rubio co-sponsored an immigration bill that provided a path to citizenship for illegals. Tea Party Opposition forced Rubio to vote against his own immigration bill. Support for minority rights is incompatible with Republican Party principles. Donald Trump talked himself into a corner. He is desperate not to lose.

The only solution for a man without a plan or a policy is to attack the opponent. That is why the people in the fever swamp of Breitbart News and Fox News want to spread rumors about Hillary Clinton's health. The bottom line of GOP Propaganda is that voters will have to take an energetic, lying, Trump, because Hillary is just too frail to serve. When you see losers like Rudy Giuliani and Sean Hannity detail the fanciful frailties of Hillary's health, you know the Trump campaign is finished.

They are losers, not because they do not make money. They make millions. They are losers because they are unprincipled opportunists, who will say anything to elect the worst candidate in U.S. History. Does anyone think that President Trump would not bring pay to play to new heights?

The character attacks against Hillary are equally without merit. Whether the GOP smear is about email,

Benghazi, or pay to play contributions to the Clinton Foundation and Clinton, Inc., for imagined State Department favors, the result is the same. There are rumors, but no evidence of culpable wrongdoing. No one knows how many emails Hillary sent and received at State. There were more than 50,000, but the public may never know the final number.

With the GOP smear machine working night and day, you might suspect that someone would come up with a list of the ten most damning emails. How about a list of 5 earthshattering emails? How about one traitorous or security violation email? Do you think Jason Chaffetz (R-UT), Chair of the House Government Oversight and Reform Committee, would not say if he had one?

The GOP wrote a speech for Pat Smith to read at the GOP convention to suggest that Hillary caused the death of Sean Smith at the U.S. Mission in Benghazi, Libya. Richard J. Cross III wrote the speech. Cross announced that he cannot vote for Trump. Giuliani, Hannity, Bannon, Ailes, and the GOP smear machine have destroyed the Republican Party.

The party of Lincoln is over. The only principle left in the GOP is 'Pay to Play'. Giuliani used to be a respected United States Attorney for the Southern District of New York. Giuliani was the beloved Mayor of New York City during the 9/11 attack. Giuliani sold his self-respect and reputation for a bowl of porridge. If it is not Rudy looking for 'Pay to Play' for himself, why is Giuliani prostituting himself by spreading false stories about Hillary's health?

The rumors are rampant in the fever swamp over 'Pay to Play' episodes allegedly involving the Clinton Foundation (CGI) and the State Department during Hillary's tenure. A manager at CGI called a high Clinton aide at State to ask if a U.S. ambassador would speak with a CGI donor.

As it turns out, the ambassador does not remember receiving any such call from the donor. Business is carried on by people speaking with other people. That is never going to change. There is nothing wrong with it. The only time there is a problem is if there is a *quid pro quo*. If Hillary wants to be effective, however, the Clintons have to sever ties with their charity.

If a CGI donor demands that State give the donor a thing of value in return for a CGI donation, that is unlawful if State gives the thing of value. In the first place, there is no evidence that State gave valuable favors to any CGI donor. In the second place, the Secretary of State does not grant State contracts. State has a team that handles contracts.

Where is the list of 10 or more contracts that State granted to CGI donors? Are there 5 such contracts? Is there even 1 such contract? Do you not think that Jason Chaffetz (R-UT) would not publicize such contracts if there were such contracts? Pay to play makes good fodder for conspiracy theorists in the fever swamp. *Quid pro quo* is difficult to show and harder to prove.

Donald Trump prides himself on winning. Now that he is losing in the polls, he is desperate. His campaign has imploded. He cannot give a policy speech on immigration because he talks out of both sides of his mouth at once. His policies consist of internally inconsistent soundbites. It is not so much that Trump is *"Dangerously Incoherent"*. He is pathological liar, whose inconsistent lies make it impossible for him to be taken seriously.

The most frightening thing about the polls is that Trump is only three or four points behind in some of the key battleground states. When a candidate's main strength is his penchant for lying, and where that candidate has no policies, and where that candidate is temperamentally unfit to be Commander-in-Chief, that candidate should be twenty points behind in the polls.

That Trump is still in the race, statistically, proves that the GOP is driven by pay to play opportunists. A Trump win could put money in the pockets of GOP Chair Reince Priebus, Hannity, Giuliani, Ailes, Christie, Bannon, and their ilk.

You can count on one hand the principled Republican luminaries who reject Trump outright. Poppy Bush, Jeb Bush, William Krystol, Susan Collins (R-ME), Lindsey Graham (R-SC), and Mitt Romney. At the GOP Convention, Ted Cruz advised delegates to vote their conscience. There is a list of 50 GOP Security Professionals who reject Trump as a threat to National Security.